PROJECT: STEAM

GROSS

SCIENCE PROJECTS

KELLY MILNER HALLS

Rourke
Educational Media

rourkeeducationalmedia.com

Before & After Reading Activities

Building Academic Vocabulary and Background Knowledge

Before reading a book, it is important to tap into what your child or students already know about the topic. This will help them develop their vocabulary, increase their reading comprehension, and make connections across the curriculum.

1. *Look at the cover of the book. What will this book be about?*
2. *What do you already know about the topic?*
3. *Let's study the Table of Contents. What will you learn about in the book's chapters?*
4. *What would you like to learn about this topic? Do you think you might learn about it from this book? Why or why not?*
5. *Use a reading journal to write about your knowledge of this topic. Record what you already know about the topic and what you hope to learn about the topic.*
6. *Read the book.*
7. *In your reading journal, record what you learned about the topic and your response to the book.*
8. *After reading the book complete the activities below.*

Content Area Vocabulary
Read the list. What do these words mean?

acetic acid
dormant
fungus
gelatin
intestines
luminescence
misshapen
moss
orbs
otherworldly
proteins
saliva
translucent

After Reading:

Comprehension and Extension Activity

After reading the book, work on the following questions with your child or students in order to check their level of reading comprehension and content mastery.

1. *How is a balloon like a drumhead?* (Summarize)
2. *Why might a moss's appearance make someone think it is dead?* (Infer)
3. *What happens when you submerge an egg in vinegar?* (Asking Questions)
4. *What's the grossest experiment you've ever done?* (Text to Self Connection)
5. *What does yeast eat?* (Asking Questions)

Extension Activity

Think about a topic you are studying in school that could be demonstrated with one of these experiments. Ask your teacher if you can bring in the materials and make the project as part of a presentation for your class.

TABLE OF CONTENTS

LET'S GET GROSS

Science can be messy—and revolting! These projects are a great way to add some fun to science explorations, from the study of the human body to the workings of volcanoes.

Make sure you have adult permission or supervision. Now let's get gross!

5

BODY FLUIDS

Fake Blood

Gather:

1. flour

2. mixing bowl

3. corn syrup

4. red & blue food coloring

5. wire whisk

6. measuring spoons

Do:

1. Put one teaspoon (5 milliliters) of flour in your mixing bowl.

2. Add a half teaspoon (2.5 milliliters) of red food coloring.

3. Add one tablespoon (15 milliliters) of corn syrup.

TIP

Wear clothes you won't mind ruining. Food coloring doesn't wash out.

4. Add one drop of blue food coloring.

5. Stir with a wire whisk until it's smooth.

6. Apply wherever you want fake blood. It's even edible, so it won't hurt you if you get it in your mouth.

Observe:

Blood has a deep scarlet tone that is captured in fake mixtures by adding a drop of blue food coloring to the mix. That's why the best fake blood recipes include that extra drop.

Fake Poop

Gather:

1. peanut butter
2. mixing bowl
3. chocolate sauce
4. plastic bag
5. spoon
6. measuring spoons
7. microwave
8. scissors

Do:

1. Put two tablespoons (32 grams) of peanut butter in your mixing bowl.

2. Mix in two tablespoons (39 grams) of chocolate sauce.

3. Stir until your mixture is all one color.

4. Microwave the mixture for 40 seconds.

5. Allow it to cool.

6. Put your mixture in a plastic bag.

7. Securely close the top of your plastic bag.

8. Cut off the corner of your plastic bag.

9. Now squeeze your fake poop out of the bag onto a plate.

Observe:

The texture of your mixture squeezing through a rounded exit point forms the perfect shape for fake poop you can eat! Be prepared for panicked looks from people who aren't in on the joke. Barf bags optional.

Fake Puke

Gather:

2. bowl

1. saltine crackers

3. warm water

4. plastic bag

5. food particles

6. corn syrup

7. microwave

Do:

1. Crush six saltine crackers into tiny bits in your plastic bag. Close the bag.

2. Add the crushed saltine pieces to the bowl.

3. Add a half cup (120 milliliters) of warm water.

4. Add tiny food bits—a sprinkle of oatmeal, finely chopped vegetables, or fruit pieces—to the mixture.

5. Add one teaspoon (5 milliliters) of clear corn syrup.

6. Microwave for 30 seconds and mix thoroughly.

TIP

If you're going to put the fake puke in your mouth, be sure to add things that taste good to your mixture. Just because it needs to LOOK gross doesn't mean it has to taste gross.

Observe:
The trick to making fake vomit look real is the texture. Real vomit is slimy because of the **saliva** and mucus in your stomach. Adding slime like corn syrup gives it a realistic ooze.

Fake Snot

Gather:

1. mixing bowl

2. water

3. corn syrup

4. fork

5. spoon

6. gelatin

7. microwave

Do:

1. Add a half cup (120 milliliters) of water to mixing bowl.

2. Microwave the water until it comes to a boil.

3. Allow the water to cool a little, but you want it warm enough to dissolve the gelatin.

4. Add three packets of gelatin, stirring gently with a fork.

5. Let it cool a bit more, then add a quarter cup (60 milliliters) of corn syrup.

6. Stir gently with the spoon and enjoy your disgusting fake snot.

Observe:

Real snot is made of **proteins** called mucin. These bond to other proteins in circular, microscopic shapes with sugar fibers jutting out like hairs toward the center of the proteins. The gelatin is also a protein. When you add water, it forms a similar molecular shape. When you add corn syrup, you're adding sugar. So it's a really good— but less disgusting— recipe for gross snotty fun.

Pop-Up Bunny Poop

Gather:

1. clear carbonated soda

2. clear glass or jar

3. raisins

Do:

1. Pour ten ounces (300 milliliters) of carbonated soda into the clear glass or jar.

2. Drop half a cup (77 grams) of raisins into the carbonated soda in the glass.

3. Watch the raisins sink to the bottom of the glass.

4. Watch the raisins pop up to the surface!

Observe:

When you drop the raisins—your bunny poop!—into carbonated soda, they sink because raisins have more density than carbonated soda. But then oxygen molecules start bonding with the raisins, making them float to the surface. When the bubbles burst, the raisins sink again.

Peanut Intestines

Gather:

1. glue

3. toilet paper

2. bowl

4. red food coloring

5. fake blood

6. needle and thread

7. packing peanuts

8. plastic tub

Do:

1. String packing peanuts end-to-end using your needle and thread.

2. Tear sheets of toilet paper into ragged shreds.

3. Pour glue into a bowl.

4. Add a drop or two of red food coloring.

5. Dip the shreds of toilet paper into the glue and wrap them around the threaded packing peanuts.

6. Repeat the same process three to five times until the string looks rubbery.

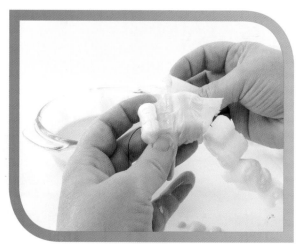

7. Let dry overnight.

8. Curl your **intestines** in a plastic tub.

9. Drench with fake blood to complete the illusion.

Observe:

Intestines are processing tubes inside the human body. The adult human body has about 25 feet (7.62 meters) of intestines coiled in the abdomen to draw nutrients from food and expel the waste.

SMELLY, STINKY STUFF

Floating Stinkers

Gather:

1. garlic clove
2. bowl
3. water
4. bubble wand
5. dish soap
6. rubbing alcohol
7. knife

Do:

1. Chop one garlic clove.
2. Add chopped garlic to your bowl.

3. Add one teaspoon (5 milliliters) of rubbing alcohol.

4. Let the alcohol and garlic sit for 30 minutes.

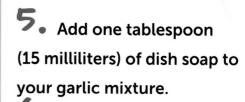

5. Add one tablespoon (15 milliliters) of dish soap to your garlic mixture.

6. Add five tablespoons (75 milliliters) of water to your garlic mixture.

7. Blow bubbles with your bubble wand and sample the smell when they pop.

8. You've mastered the magic of floating stinkers.

Observe:

Traditional bubble solution smells like soap because there are no noxious elements in the recipe for traditional bubbles. But if you add something offensive in your solution—something like garlic, onions, or stinky human sweat—that scent is captured inside the floating bubbles. When they pop, that smell is explosively released.

Soap Beast

Gather:

2. microwave-safe plate

1. Ivory brand soap bar

3. microwave oven

Do:

1. Place small bar (or a quarter of a full-size bar) of fresh Ivory soap on a microwave-safe plate. It must be Ivory and it must be fresh.

2. Put the plate and soap in your microwave.

3. Heat on high for one to two minutes.

4. Watch your monster take shape!

TIP

Be careful when you take your soap monster out of the microwave because it will be very hot. But once it cools, explore the fragile, breakable texture of the expanded soap.

Observe:

Ivory soap is famous because it floats! It floats because it is filled with tiny air bubbles. It is also full of moisture. When you heat the soap, the moisture expands and the soap expands with it to create a creepy, **misshapen** soap monster.

29

Burping Bottle

Gather:

1. water

2. glass soda bottle

3. straw

4. dime

5. freezer

Do:

1. Gently balance a dime over the mouth of an empty glass soda bottle.

2. Place the bottle with the dime covering the mouth into the freezer.

3. Allow to stand in the freezer for three to four hours.

4. Carefully remove the bottle from the freezer without knocking the dime off.

5. Fill a glass or cup about a quarter full with water.

6. Wrap one hand around the body of the bottle.

7. Drip water on the dime using a straw (place the straw in a glass of water, put your thumb over the top of the straw and water will be trapped inside the straw).

8. Watch carefully as the bottle begins to burp, lifting the dime off the mouth very slightly.

Observe:

Air is trapped in the empty bottle by the dime covering the mouth. When you place that bottle in the freezer, the air drops in temperature. As you remove the bottle and wrap your hand around the bottle, the air inside gets warmer. Warmer air expands and escapes as a "burp" at the mouth of the bottle, lifting the dime.

Fart Foam

Gather:

1. small jar or glass

2. yeast

3. warm water

4. sugar

Do:

1. Pour 0.75 ounce (21 gram) of yeast into your jar or glass.

2. Add one teaspoon (5 milliliters) of sugar. Mix well.

3. Add two tablespoons (30 milliliters) of very warm water.

4. Wait ten minutes.

5. Take a whiff of your fart foam.

Observe:

Yeast is a living organism called a **fungus**. It loves to eat sugar. When you add warm water to the dry yeast, it wakes up hungry. When it eats the sugar, gas called carbon dioxide is formed. That gas makes your fart foam stinky!

CREEPY, ICKY, YUCK

Icky Egg Transformation

Gather:

3. vinegar

2. glass

1. uncooked egg

Do:

1. Fill a glass three-quarters full with vinegar.

2. Carefully pick up an uncooked egg.

3. Put the egg in the glass of vinegar.

4. Let the egg and vinegar stand for 24 hours.

5. Very gently drain the vinegar, being careful not to let the egg fall into the sink.

6. Gently squeeze the egg and you'll find the egg shell has softened to a rubbery texture.

7. Be sure to dispose of the egg carefully outside. It will decompose quickly leaving an unpleasant smell in your indoor trash can.

Observe:

Vinegar is about four percent **acetic acid**. When you submerge an egg in vinegar, a chemical reaction dissolves the shell made of calcium carbonate, leaving it rubbery and **translucent**.

It's ALIVE!

Gather:

1. blender

2. water

3. clean disposable diaper

4. **moss** (orchid or frog moss available in craft or hardware stores)

5. buttermilk

6. measuring spoons

7. paintbrush

8. bucket

9. squirt bottle filled with water

Do:

1. Pour a quarter cup (60 milliliters) of buttermilk into the blender.

2. Pour one and one-half cups (350 milliliters) of water into the blender.

37

3. Add two clumps of dry moss to the blender.

4. Remove the water-absorbent powder from the clean diaper.

5. Add two teaspoons (10 milliliters) of the powder to the blender.

6. Blend mixture thoroughly and pour into a bucket.

7. Use your paintbrush to paint a friendly message on a sunny wall outside. Caution: this mixture can dissolve paint, so ask before you use a space for this experiment.

8. Mist your message with a squirt bottle every day until it starts to grow—and several days a week if you want it to stay ALIVE!

Observe:

Some mosses seem dead, but they are actually **dormant**. They are waiting for the return of water to sprout again. When you combine that dry moss with the right materials, it reawakens and will grow in the right circumstances. Why add diaper powder? To retain the water you spray on your outdoor message and encourage growth.

Ghostly Orbs

Gather:

1. clear glass bowl

2. water

3. bag of Jelly Beadz

4. measuring spoon

5. glow powder

6. blacklight or dark room

Do:

1. Pour about half a bag of Jelly Beadz into a clear glass bowl.

2. Add about eight and a half cups (2 liters) of water to the bowl. Use less if your bowl is too small.

3. Allow the water and Jelly Beadz to soak overnight.

4. Add one tablespoon (15 milliliters) of glow powder to the mixture.

5. Expose your bead mixture to strong light for two hours and darken the room for a glimpse of your ghostly **orbs**. Or, darken the room and turn on a blacklight and swirl the mixture for spooky, glowing fun.

Observe:

Jelly Beadz absorb water overnight and expand in size. They also seem to disappear in what's left of the water. The glow powder adds **luminescence** to the mix to make your orbs glow in the dark or under a blacklight.

41

Volcanic Wax

Gather:

1. water

2. large heat-resistant cup or Pyrex beaker

3. fine-grain sand

4. colored tealight candle or wax chunk (a darker color is better)

5. hot plate or stove burner

Do:

1. Place the wax into the cup or beaker.

2. Cover the wax with the sand.

3. Fill the cup or beaker with clean, fresh water, leaving just half an inch (1.27 centimeters) of space at the top.

4. Allow the mixture to settle and clear.

5. Place the cup or beaker on the hot plate or stove burner.

6. Heat to medium-high temperature.

7. Watch your eruption begin.

8. Turn the heat off and allow the cup or beaker to cool completely before you clean up your experiment.

Observe:

As the heat melts the wax buried beneath the sand, it bursts through the soil in a thin stream, like lava, and rises to the top of the water. Why the top? Wax floats when it's not weighted down with sand.

Wailing Wobbler

Gather:

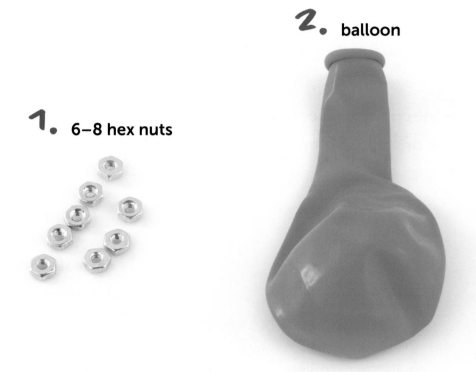

2. balloon

1. 6–8 hex nuts

Do:

1. Put six to eight hex nuts inside the empty balloon.

2. Blow it up.

3. Tie it off.

4. Now rapidly swirl the balloon as you hold it firmly in your hand.

5. Listen closely for the **otherworldly** wailing wobblers!

Observe:

Like a drumhead, balloons are stretched materials. Hit a drum and you'll hear a deep rumble. Hit a balloon with the metal points of six-sided, hexagon-shaped nuts and you'll hear higher-pitched thumps.

GLOSSARY

acetic acid (as-SEH-tik a-sihd): a colorless, strong smelling acid found in organic liquids like vinegar

dormant (DOR-muhnt): living thing that is alive but inactive—as if asleep until conditions change to bring it back to active growth

fungus (FUHN-guhs): a plant-like living organism that has no leaves, flowers, roots or chlorophyll and grows on other plants, dead or living

gelatin (JEL-uh-tin): a clear substance made from animal bones and tissues used in making glue, Jello and marshmallows

intestines (in-TES-tins): a long tube in living bodies that digests food

luminescence (loo-muh-NEH-sens): the emission of light without a heat source

misshapen (mis-SHAYP-en): not having a normal or natural shape

moss (maws): a small, fuzzy plant that grows on soil, rocks and tree bark

orbs (orbz): circular objects, including bursts of light

otherworldly (uhTH-ur-wurld-lee): from an imaginary, spiritual or mysterious place, not of Earth

proteins (PROH-teens): types of chemical compounds found in living cells, such as plants and animals

saliva (suh-LYE-vuh): the watery fluid in your mouth that softens your food and keeps your mouth moist

translucent (trans-LOO-suhnt): a substance that is not clear like glass, but does let some light through

INDEX

SHOW WHAT YOU KNOW

1. What is yeast?
2. Is sugar a part of human snot?
3. What is mucin?
4. How many sides are in a hexagon?
5. Why do raisins sink in carbonated soda?

FURTHER READING

Winterbottom, Julie, and Bozek, Rachel, *Frightlopedia: An Encyclopedia of Everything Scary, Creepy, and Spine-Chilling, from Arachnids to Zombies*, Workman Publishing, 2016.

Ahlquist, Jon, and Wheeler-Toppen, Jodi Lyn, *Gross Science Projects*, Capstone Press, 2013.

Massoff, Joy, *Oh, Ick!: 114 Science Experiments Guaranteed to Gross You Out!*, Workman Publishing Company, 2016.

ABOUT THE AUTHOR

Kelly Milner Halls is a writer best known for being weird. She loves all things gross, including *Mad Magazine* and alien invaders. When she's not writing, Kelly explores life's mysteries in Spokane, Washington, where she lives with two daughters, too many cats, a Great Dane and a four-foot-long rock iguana named Gigantor. She hopes to meet a Bigfoot someday!

www.rourkeeducationalmedia.com

PHOTO CREDITS: Cover & all pages: © creativelytara; Page 4: © Django; Page 5: © Allkindza; Page 27: © drbimages, © fer3250

Edited by: Keli Sipperley
Cover and Interior design by: Tara Raymo *www.creativelytara.com*

Library of Congress PCN Data

Gross Science Projects / Kelly Milner Halls
(Project: STEAM)
ISBN 978-1-64156-466-3 (hard cover)(alk. paper)
ISBN 978-1-64156-592-9 (soft cover)
ISBN 978-1-64156-708-4 (e-Book)
Library of Congress Control Number: 2018930492

Printed in the United States of America, North Mankato, Minnesota

Rourke Educational Media
Printed in the United States of America,
North Mankato, Minnesota